VIKING GODS! FROM ODIN TO THOR

VIKINGS FOR KIDS

Children's Exploration & Discovery History Books

Left Brain Kids

Educational Books for Children

Meet the mighty Viking,
or Norse, gods

Discover interesting facts
about Viking gods

Kids, in this book you will get amazing facts about the Viking gods. Read on and be fascinated by their power and strength.

See what each god can do!

One of the people of Scandinavia were called Vikings. They believed in many gods.

The Viking gods were originally two groups of gods in Norse mythology. The first group is known as Aesir, or the sky gods, and are worshiped for war and victory.

The second group is known as Vanir, or the earth gods, and are worshiped for prosperity and the harvest from the earth. They were also known as wise and skillful in magical arts.

These two groups were thought to have waged war on each other. They made peace on the condition of a prisoner exchange.

The Viking or Norse Gods

Odin – meet the Father of all the gods! The god of wisdom and war He is called the All-father. He is the king of the gods and the wisest of the Viking gods.

He usually disguised himself on his travels by wearing masks and a green coat. That is why he comes with 36 different names. Odin was the son of the ancestor of the Aesir family known as Bor.

Thor - meet the son of Odin and earth! The protector of mankind and the god of thunder

He is the most famous son of Odin. Thor is considered as the strongest of all the Viking gods. His weapon is a hammer known as Miolnir and he can make thunder by using it.

He also possesses a powerful belt that increases his strength when he wears it. He uses a pair of iron gloves as he holds his hammer. These three things double his strength.

Freyr - Meet the god of fertility! The god of generosity He is the son of Niord. He is considered as one of the greatest Viking gods. He is known to control the prosperity of men and the fruits of the earth.

The sunshine and the rain are under his control. He owns a boar known as Gullinbursti

Balder - meet the wisest of all the Viking gods! He is the son of Odin and Frigg. His home in heaven is known as Breidablik, or far shining. He also owns the greatest of all ships, known as **Hringhorn**.

He is known as the most gentle of the Viking gods, but is plagued by bad dreams. He is the god of the summer sun. For his radiance, he is known as a being of great beauty.

Niord – meet the wealthy god! He can give land and money to anyone. He is known to control people's prosperity and wealth, but originally he was the god of fertility. He is the god of the seas according to Icelandic sources.

Tyr – meet the bravest of the Viking gods! He is the son of Odin. He is capable of deciding the outcome of battles. He is known to be very wise and far-sighted.

Heimdall- meet the guardian of the gods! He is another son of Odin. He is also known as the **white god** and **Goldtooth**.

He lives in Himinbjorg or heaven rock. He has exceptional senses of sight and hearing.

Loki- meet the trickster god! He is a minor god. He is known as a **shape-shifter.** He can transform into different animals. He committed various crimes against the gods, including causing Baldur's death.

The Viking gods live in place known as Asgard. This palace is in the sky and is made of gold and silver.

These Viking gods have their own personalities and amazing adventures. They are also called as the gods of the north.

They are not immortals, but they do have magical powers and they live longer than ordinary people.

Manufactured by Amazon.ca
Bolton, ON

16905211R00026